Hope for your HOME

Dr. Don Brawley III
Mona L. Brawley
Founding Pastors of Canaan Land Church Intl.

Canaan Land Church International
PO Box 390820
Snellville, GA 30039
www.canaanlandchurch.org

Content includes Scripture passages from the HOLY BIBLE, including the New International Version (NIV), King James Version (KJV), New King James Version (NKJV), New Living Translation (NLT), New American Standard Bible (NASB), English Standard Version (ESV), and The Message (MSG).

CREDITS:
Curriculum Writing Team and Editors:
Natoshia Anderson, Odell Anderson, Joseph Arnold, Brandon Brawley, Mona Brawley, Vince Carter, Amanda Davis, Ann Farrow, and Esther Mention

Photo Selections Team: Aaron Brawley, Amanda Davis, and Cameryn Farrow

Photographer: Leonard Kinsey (leonardkinseyphotography.com)

Additional images from Shutterstock.com

ISBN#: 978-0-9971692-0-1
Library of Congress Control Number: 2016930038

Printed in the United States of America

TABLE OF CONTENTS

3

ACKNOWLEDGMENTS

Canaan Land Church we are humbled to shepherd you and honored to call you family! Thank you for your steadfast support, infectious generosity, and undying commitment. Without your support, creating this study wouldn't have been possible.

We'd like to acknowledge our parents, Don Brawley Jr., Desiree S. Brawley, Charles B. Frazier, Sr., and Betty Frazier Settles for their unspoken sacrifice, examples of parenthood, and the gift of family they bestowed upon us.

Our greatest gratitude is for our Lord and Savior Jesus Christ, who made us part of His eternal family and is the Living Hope that we share with one another and our children: Aaron, Chantelle, Brandon and daughter-in-love Kristie.

INTRODUCTION

Studies, news reports, and even popular culture have shown that families of every race in the U.S. have suffered breakdown since the 1950s. However, Black families have suffered more from the breakdown of family than all other races in America. In 1950, 78% of all households were married; female-headed households made up only 8% of that total. The number of married households has declined drastically over the decades—only 48% of all households are currently married. Moreover, the number of female-headed households has risen to 12%[1]. For Black families, 17% were headed by women in 1950[2].

Today that number has climbed to 29%, more than double the number for all families[3]. Black men are almost six times more likely to be incarcerated than white men, and 60% of all prisoners in the U.S. are people of color[4]. If white American families have a cold, Black American families have severe pneumonia! Certainly all families matter; however, given the current state of Black America and its families, awareness must shine on the seemingly not so obvious: Black Families Matter.

The "Black Lives Matter" movement was co-organized in the summer of 2012 by three Black women—Patrisse Cullors, Opal Tomeit, and Alicia Garza—after the acquittal of George Zimmerman in the shooting death of Black teenager Trayvon Martin. Since then the movement has quickly gained traction, attracted media attention, and increased its following. While this study is not an endorsement for or against this movement, nor is it in any way affiliated with it, we feel it only appropriate that we acknowledge the

5

"It is our belief that Black lives will not matter tomorrow unless Black families matter today. The Bible shows us the family was the first institution created by God. ... As a community of faith, we believe faith in Jesus Christ is essential to lasting personal and community transformation."

movement's founders since we are using a variation of their phrase in our trilogy title, "Black Families Matter."

It is our belief that Black lives will not matter tomorrow unless Black families matter today. The Bible shows us the family was the first institution created by God. Sociology shows us that family is the basic unit of society. In addition, history shows us that strong families make strong civilizations. Without the strength of fortified Black families, Black lives will remain vulnerable to societal, systemic, and even our own self-inflicted brokenness.

As a community of faith, we believe faith in Jesus Christ is essential to lasting personal and community transformation. It is our prayer that the interactions within your group coupled with the teachings within this trilogy will restore hope, release healing, and rebuild our families and community.

We're glad you joined us for this three-part journey "Black Families Matter": Hope for Your Home; Healing for Your Home; and Help for Your Home (It Takes a Village). We look forward to seeing you and hearing about all God has done for you and your family as we embark on this exciting journey together.

USING THIS WORKBOOK

Tools to Help You Have a Great Small Group Experience!

Notice in the Table of Contents that after the sessions, there are two additional key sections:

- Appendices
- Small Group Leaders.

Familiarize yourself with the Appendices. Some of the contents will be used during the sessions.

1. If you are facilitating/leading or co-leading a small group, the section Small Group Leaders will encourage you by giving you a solid blueprint on how to effectively lead groups, including how to avoid common mistakes that others have learned the hard way.
2. Use this workbook as a guide. If the group responds to a lesson in an unexpected but honest way, go with that. If you think of a question other than the next one in the lesson, ask it. Take to heart the insights included in the Frequently Asked Questions pages and the Small Group Leaders section.
3. Enjoy your small group experience. Have fun.
4. Pray before each session—for your group members, for your time together, and for your wisdom and insights.
5. Read the Outline for Each Session on the following pages so that you understand how the sessions will flow.

OUTLINE OF EACH SESSION

A typical session for the "Hope for Your Home" study will include the following sections:

INTRODUCTION (2 MINUTES SUGGESTED):

Each lesson opens with a brief thought that will help you prepare for the session and get you thinking about the particular subject you will explore with your group. Make it a practice to read these before the session.

OPEN UP (20 MINUTES SUGGESTED):

The foundation for spiritual growth is an intimate connection with God and God's family. You build that connection by sharing your experience with a few people who really know you and who earn your trust. This is helpful preparation for being able to share what Christ has done in your life with anyone you meet, which is what a disciple is ready to do. This section includes some simple questions to get you talking, letting you share as much or as little of your story as you feel comfortable doing. Each section typically offers you two options: You can get to know your whole group by using the icebreaker question(s), or you can check in with one or two group members—your spiritual partner(s)—for a deeper connection and encouragement in your spiritual journey.

TAKE IT IN (12 MINUTES SUGGESTED):

Each week, we will watch a video with Pastors Don and Mona for the session. Space is provided to take notes.

TALK IT OVER (20 MINUTES SUGGESTED):

In this section, you'll read the Bible and reflect together on the teaching. Take turns reading the questions and make the decision to participate in the conversation.

WORK IT OUT (20 MINUTES SUGGESTED):

During this section, the focus will be on personal application, helping one another see how the insights from the teaching and the Scripture can affect life where we live it and lead us to discovering hope for our homes. There will also be some time for quiet reflection.

MOVE IT FORWARD:

God wants you to be a part of His kingdom—to weave your story into His story. That will mean change. It will require you to go His way rather than your own. This will not happen overnight, but it should happen steadily. By making small, simple choices, we can begin to change our direction. This is where the Bible's instructions to "be doers of the Word, not just hearers" (James 1:22) come into play. Many people skip over this aspect of the Christian life because it's scary, relationally awkward, or simple too much work for their busy schedules. But Jesus wanted all of His disciples to know Him personally, carry out His commands, and help others connect with Him. This doesn't necessarily mean preaching on street corners. It could mean welcoming newcomers, hosting a short-term small group, or walking through this study with a friend. In this study, you'll have an opportunity to go beyond Bible study to biblical living.

DEEPER STUDY:

This section provides additional Scriptures and commentary to take you even deeper into the main topic of each section.

REFLECT ON IT:

Each week, we're including Scriptures to read and reflect upon between sessions. This provides you with the chance to slow down, read just a small portion of Scripture each day, and reflect and pray through it. You will then have a chance to journal your response to what you read. Use this section to seek God on your own throughout the week. This time at home should begin and end with prayer. Try not to be in a hurry. Take enough time to hear God's direction.

BLACK FAMILIES MATTER
HOPE FOR YOUR HOME

SESSION 1

"Your Family Matters to God"

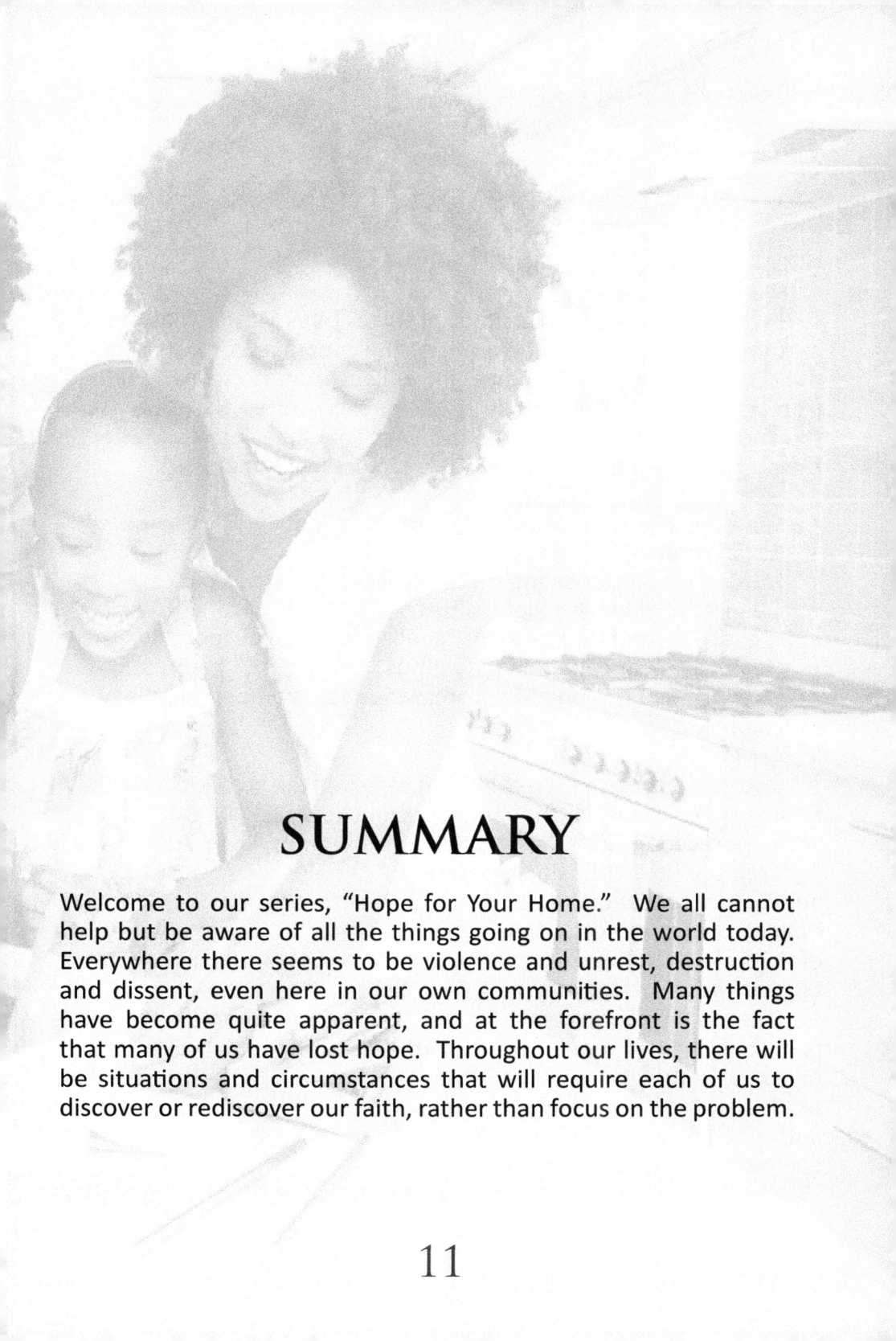

SUMMARY

Welcome to our series, "Hope for Your Home." We all cannot help but be aware of all the things going on in the world today. Everywhere there seems to be violence and unrest, destruction and dissent, even here in our own communities. Many things have become quite apparent, and at the forefront is the fact that many of us have lost hope. Throughout our lives, there will be situations and circumstances that will require each of us to discover or rediscover our faith, rather than focus on the problem.

INTRODUCTION

HOUSTON... WE HAVE A PROBLEM!!!

In the recent media, the message "Black Lives Matter" has become a mantra and a movement. In fact, the message is reminiscent of the "Save the Whales" campaign, which promoted saving whales from extinction! This fact only further illustrates the direness of the situation. The need for the message that "Black Lives Matter" is fueled by ever-present and systemic factors including:

- Search and frisk of people of color
- Racial profiling
- Massive unemployment and underemployment
- Generational wealth inequalities
- Welfare system that rewards families for male absence
- Health and educational inequalities
- Over-criminalization and incarceration rates among people of color

Over time, these harsh realities have fueled the breakdown of Black families. For example, the family nucleus itself has been torn apart with unprecedented fatherlessness in our homes. Over 70% of Black children are born into single-parent households, compared to white and Latino households at 25% and 50% respectively[3]. Black families headed by single mothers with children under 18 have a poverty rate of 47.5%[5]. At first look, these problems can seem insurmountable, but we know nothing is too hard for God!

Despite the problems within our families and communities, Jesus is looking for His people to find faith in His ability to work through us to solve our problems. No matter what our present perils may be, Jesus is still able and ready to partner with those who, through faith in Him, are willing to see a new reality in their lives, homes, communities, and the world.

We hope that you will use this study as a spiritual and practical

12

tool in a greater arsenal to solve the systemic problems we face individually and collectively.

Welcome to the beginning of the journey ... Hope for Your Home.

OPEN UP

Heavenly Father, thank you for bringing us each here today to walk in this journey of "Hope for Your Home." Lord, God, we know that Jesus said that in this world we would have trouble but be of good courage for I have overcome the world. Thank you that, despite living in a world plagued by so many troubles, we find faith and hope in you. Be with us as we walk this journey as a group and individually as your children, for you have promised to never leave or forsake us. And it is in that promise that we set forward on this journey of faith, hope, and love. In Jesus's name we pray, Amen.

1. What are you expecting God to do for you or your family during our "Hope for Your Home" journey?
2. It is a fact that the family structure in society is broken. How has that brokenness spread into your home and family, directly or indirectly?
3. Understanding what brokenness looks like, what are some beginning steps that we can take to start the journey towards bringing hope back to the family at large and that you can take in your own home?

TAKE IT IN: DVD SESSION

Watch the DVD for this session now. We have provided a space for Notes. There you can record any key thoughts, questions, and things you want to remember or follow up on. After watching the video, have someone read the discussion questions in the "Talk It Over" section and direct the discussion among the group. As you go through each of the subsequent sections, ask someone else to read the questions and direct the discussion.

TALK IT OVER

In today's video, Pastor Brawley spoke of John 9:1-5 about the man born blind and how most individuals were looking for the cause or fault to lay blame. In the end, Jesus teaches us that the man's blindness was but a way for God's glory to be shown. You see, the disciples were looking to find fault, but Jesus was looking to find faith! Similarly today, we believe His disciples—whether Black, white, or other—are challenged to do the same.

4. Talk to your group about a time when you put your hope in something or someone else that disappointed you, only to find out that you really needed to put your hope in God.
5. The mantra "Black Lives Matter" can be found throughout the news and social media. What does this say about the state of our society, the Black community, and the Black family—that it has to be specifically stated that Black lives matter?
6. As we discussed earlier in this session, Black lives are far more vulnerable to the systemic illnesses of society. What are some of the systemic illnesses that you can identify in your life?
7. In what ways can hope become a "vaccination" to protect our families against the illnesses of society?
8. The focus of this series is "Hope for Your Home." In this session, we've talked about the feelings of hopelessness in Black families often due to placing our hope in the wrong places. Simply put, our hope has been misplaced. Tell of a time when you misplaced your hope from being in God to something or someone else. Did you find your way back to hoping in God. If so, tell how.

14

WALK IT OUT

Just as in the Scripture story of the blind man and the disciples, Jesus is looking for faith (John 9:3). It is our faith in Jesus that will solve the systemic problems that our families face on a daily basis. The Duke University study that Pastor Brawley discussed proves that hope sustains life. You don't have to be hopeless when you place your hope in Jesus. He is the sustainer of all things and He is "the life."

Unfortunately, many people don't know that yet. So they remain hopeless. With each injustice they witness, unanswered outcry they watch on the evening news, and failed promises from elected officials, little seems to change. Although each of these attempts may have merit, they are ever changing and therefore aren't sufficient to maintain our hope. Instead, we should trust in our living God alone who never changes and is more than capable of sustaining our hope and supplying our needs.

He has already made provision for you and your family. Just as in the Scripture story of Hagar and Ishmael, it was when Ishmael cried out that God answered his cry. God knows all the things that will happen in your life, and He will make provisions, as Hagar learned. In the story, God had provision for Hagar and Ishmael, yet Hagar was hopelessly awaiting death. It wasn't until her son cried out that God answered. Sometimes God doesn't open your eyes to what He has for your family until someone in your family cries out. Maybe the person He is waiting for to cry out for your family is YOU!

When you cry out, God shows that his provisions are greater than your problems. Just like Hagar, we've placed our babies under a bush waiting

15

NOTES

NOTES

for the government, the schools, lawmakers, law enforcement, courts, affirmative action, celebrities... but there is no one better to trust and put your hope in than God. He already knows where you will be before you get there. Moreover, He has already supplied the water you need to sustain your family members and move them forward.

9. Throughout our session, we have talked about the significance of hope. Share a time when your family's strength of hope proved itself clear.
10. What would it look like for you to "cry out" to God for your family? Have you ever cried out before? What happened?
11. We all have the ability to be a light to our loved ones. Just as Ishmael's cries were heard by God, and brought God's provision, so can each one of us be a light in our own homes. Specifically what can you do to be a light to those in your family?
12. Faith is the very basis of our relationship with a living God. What does faith mean to you? How do you see faith, as an action word, being shown or rather done?

MOVE IT FORWARD

This week, take what you learned and spend some time putting it into practice. Choose one or more of the following activities to further your spiritual growth and even connect with others in your group. Don't feel you have to complete all of these. Decide what you can commit to and go for it. Consider sharing your experiences the next time you meet with the group.

18

PRAY FOR EACH OTHER THIS WEEK.
You can use the Prayer and Praise Report gathered earlier in this meeting to support your group in prayers.

REFLECT ON IT.
Commit to daily connection with God. See suggestions on how to do this each day in the "Reflect On It" section.

CHANGE YOUR MIND.
Memorizing Scripture helps to redirect our minds to God's plan. Take time to give this important practice a try.

2 Samuel 7:18 (NIV)
"...Who am I, Sovereign LORD, and what is my family, that you have brought me this far?"

DEEPER STUDY

I knew a lady who raised her granddaughter in a faith-based Christian home. However, there came a time in her life when she thought all hope was gone. She was lonely and felt defeated. She lived in one room with black window dressings. She even considered herself an atheist.

One day, when she was at her lowest, she cried out to God because she needed a job. Within one week she had so many job offers that she had to make a choice. While she was working two of the jobs she had chosen, she applied for a job with New York State. She had to attend several classes and take a final exam, which she passed with a high score.

Now she has a permanent state job with a decent salary and benefits. She moved into her own apartment with bright window dressings, and she bought a reliable car. Most of all, she no longer sees herself as an atheist. She gives God the glory!!! She is working on her relationship with Jesus, and she realizes that she didn't lose hope; she just misplaced it.

1. Think of a time when you thought all hope was lost. Explain. Tell how God restored your faith.

According to Baker's Evangelical Dictionary of Biblical Theology, to hope is to trust in, wait for, or desire something or someone; or expect something beneficial in the future.

The Bible says:
"Now faith is the substance of things hoped for, the evidence of things not seen." Hebrews 11:1 (KJV)

Read Psalm 25: 2-3 (KJV)
"O my God, I trust in thee: let me not be ashamed, let not mine enemies triumph over me. Yea, let none that wait on thee be ashamed: let them be ashamed which transgress without cause."

2. In this passage what word can be translated as hope?

Read Psalm 25:21, 27:14, 40:1, 130:5-7 (KJV)

Psalm 25:21
"Let integrity and uprightness preserve me; for I wait on thee."

Psalm 27:14
"Wait on the LORD: be of good courage, and he shall strengthen thine heart: wait, I say, on the LORD."

Psalm 40:1
"I waited patiently for the LORD; and he inclined unto me, and heard my cry."

Psalm 130:5-7
"I wait for the LORD, my soul doth wait, and in his word do I hope. My soul waiteth for the Lord more than they that watch for the morning: I say, more than they that watch for the morning. Let Israel hope in the LORD: for with the LORD there is mercy, and with him is plenteous redemption."

3. According to these Scriptures, when you are feeling hopeless and uncertain, what should you do?
4. Share with your group a time when your faith was increased because something you hoped for came to pass.
5. How can you apply that increased faith to situations in your family, your church, or your community?

The definition for hope implies that there is a waiting period.

6. What are you doing while you wait? Instead of waiting for institutions and officials, are you asking God how you can use your time and God-given talent to get the job done?

James 2:20 (KJV)
"But wilt thou know, O vain man, that faith without works is dead?"

Suggestions:

• Join a small group in your church.
• Join the PTA at your child's school.
• Volunteer at your child's school.
• Join neighborhood watch.
• Organize or attend neighborhood meetings.

REFLECT ON IT

Daily Verses

Day 1

Scripture: Psalm 33:22
"Let your unfailing love surround us, Lord, for our hope is in you alone." (NLT)

Observation
Our hope must be in God alone. His love is what sustains and protects us.

Application
What does it mean to put all our hope in God? What does that look like?

Day 2

Scripture: Proverbs 23:18
"You will be rewarded for this; your hope will not be disappointed." (NLT)

Observation
God understands what it means for each of us to put our hope in Him alone. With that knowledge, He reassures us that our hope is not in vain and that we will be rewarded.

Application
What does the Scripture say about God's assured grace towards us and patience? Reflect on a time when God has reassured your hope in Him.

Day 3

Scripture: Romans 15:3-4
"... As the Scriptures say, 'The insults of those who insult you,
O God, have fallen on me.' Such things were written in the
Scriptures long ago to teach us. And the Scriptures give us hope
and encouragement as we wait patiently for God's promises to be
fulfilled." (NLT)

Observation
There are those that will insult and place blame. God knows this and
all things. He instructs us to stay patient and steadfast in knowing
that all that He has promised will be fulfilled.

Application
How has God helped you find patience? What are God's promises
for you?

Day 4

Scripture: Ephesians 4:4-6
"For there is one body and one Spirit, just as you have been called
to one glorious hope for the future. There is one Lord, one faith,
one baptism, one God and Father of all, who is over all, in all, and
living through all." (NLT)

Observation
There is only one true God.

Application
Knowing that God alone is Lord, how does that affect your outlook
of the future for yourself? Your family?

23

Day 5

Scripture: Romans 15:13
"I pray that God, the source of hope, will fill you completely with joy and peace because you trust in him. Then you will overflow with confident hope through the power of the Holy Spirit." (NLT)

Observation
God is the source of all hope. Therefore, there are direct links between our faith and trust in Him and the hope we feel in our lives.

Application
How has your trust in God brought you hope? Hope for your family?

Day 6

Summary
Use this space to write any thoughts God has put in your heart and mind about hope for your home.

BLACK FAMILIES MATTER
HOPE FOR YOUR HOME

SESSION 2

"You Are Worth More"

SUMMARY

You have immeasurable and eternal value to God.

INTRODUCTION

There are times in our lives when we feel as though we have been forgotten—times when we have asked, "God what am I doing wrong? God do you hear me?" Just like the $20 bills that Pastor Brawley spoke of, no matter where you have been, how you have been handled, you have a story. Oftentimes because of social status, employment status, relationship status, educational background, credit report rating, criminal record, things we have done or failed to do, we feel as though we are not as worthy as others. No matter your history, you are worthy in the eyes of God. Luke 12:6-7 says, "For you are worth more than many sparrows." Therefore, we know that no matter what may come, your value, in God's eyes, never depreciates.

OPEN UP

Dear Lord, we come to you in thanks for this opportunity to come together. We, as a group, agree to purposefully search for your voice and the conscious fulfillment of your will. We know that all things work for our good and that our greatest gift in this life is to give you the praise and glory. Almighty God, keep us close, and may we continue to search diligently for your face in all we do. In Jesus's Holy name, Amen.

Questions for Small Groups

1. Give an example of a time in your life when you questioned your value.
2. What role does value currently play in your life? What does that same value mean for you in respect to God and life everlasting?
3. It's not too late to invite others to participate in this small group. Each of us has a sphere of influence that we need to pray for and

keep in mind as we study "Hope for Your Home." In one way or another they are on this path with us. Take a look at the Circles of Life diagram and write the names of two or three people you know who need to know Christ. Commit to praying for God's guidance and an opportunity to share with each of them.

CIRCLES OF LIFE

DISCOVER WHO YOU CAN CONNECT IN THE COMMUNITY

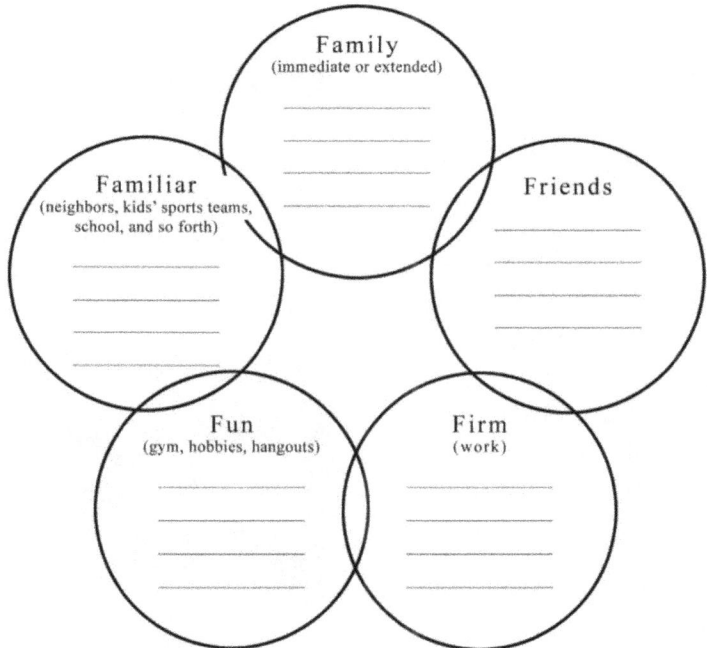

Follow this simple four-step process:

1. Prayerfully list 1-2 people in each circle.
2. Prepare the group for them. Share a few names with your group and update your progress.
3. Place a call to them.
4. Pick them up and bring them to your next meeting.

"Follow me, and I will make you fishers of men." Matthew 4:19

29

TAKE IT IN: DVD SESSION

Watch the DVD for this session now. We have provided a space for Notes. There you can record any key thoughts, questions, and things you want to remember or follow up on. After watching the video, have someone read the discussion questions in the "Talk It Over" section and direct the discussion among the group. As you go through each of the subsequent sections, ask someone else to read the questions and direct the discussion.

TALK IT OVER

Do you realize how deeply God loves you? In the passage from Luke, we learn about five sparrows bought for two coins. Now the story is that two sparrows could be bought for one coin. This means that one sparrow, the fifth one, did not have any value but was merely an extra for purchase. But be not afraid, for that fifth sparrow is just as valuable and is not forgotten in His sight. He has numbered each individual hair on your head. God knows everything about you, not just the number of hairs but also where each follicle is on your head. Isn't God amazing!!! It's because He knows us so individually and specifically that we know that He loves us intentionally and constantly.

To truly understand the enormity of God's love, you have to realize that this is the same God of the Universe. He oversees the movement of the planets, the coming and going of the seasons, and all of life's mysteries. This same great and powerful God is watching over you and me, every day, morning and night. The Scripture says, "Not one of them is forgotten at any time before God." You are worth more to God individually AND collectively.

1. Have you perceived your value as something that changes based on your circumstances or something that remains steady despite them? Explain.
2. To you, what does it mean for God to have given His only begotten Son for your salvation? What does that say to you about how much God cherishes you?
3. Knowing the depth of God's love for you, how can you show God your love for Him?

WALK IT OUT

Consider this: When God made each of us, He took into consideration our failure, our sin, our imperfection, our shame, and our doubt, saying when "I came to redeem you, the only one that could redeem you was the only one with the same value as you, my ONLY begotten Son." Your righteousness is defined by God's giving—completely, and without question—His only Son. This is a testament to your life's value.

You are very valuable to God. Now as you continue your discussion, think about the value that your life has to God. Examine your life through the lenses of God's unending and unyielding love. God bless you and have a great discussion.

4. Knowing that there is nothing God would not do for you, what would/will you do for God?
5. Sacrifice. That is at the very basis of God's love for us. Sacrifice

NOTES

NOTES

is seen at the fundamental basis of all relationships. Speak of a time when you have sacrificed for another as an act of love, not for acknowledgement or credit, but solely out of love and admiration.

MOVE IT FORWARD

This week, take what you learned and spend some time putting it into practice. Choose one or more of the following activities to further your spiritual growth and even connect with others in your group. Don't feel you have to complete all of these. Decide what you can commit to and go for it. Consider sharing your experiences the next time you meet with the group.

PRAY FOR EACH OTHER THIS WEEK.
You can use the Prayer and Praise Report gathered earlier in this meeting to support your group in prayer. Check back about requests to see how God is answering prayers.

REFLECT ON IT.
Commit to daily connection with God. See suggestions on how to do that each day in the "Reflect On It" section. Try using the S.O.A.P. method.

CHANGE YOUR MIND.
Memorizing Scripture helps to redirect our minds to God's plan. Take time to give this important practice a try.

Matthew 10:31 (NIV)
"So don't be afraid; you are worth more than many sparrows."

DEEPER STUDY

Read Genesis 37: The story of Joseph's young life

Verses 3-4: Tell how Jacob loved Joseph more than any of his other sons, because he was born to him in his old age. Jacob made an ornate robe for Joseph. When Joseph's brothers saw that their father loved him more than any of them, they hated him.

Verses 5-7: A dream is what turns his brothers violent. Joseph, age seventeen, tells his family he had a dream that the sun, moon, and 11 stars bowed before him. Even old Jacob gets upset about that because he sees the symbolism.

1. Do you think that Joseph confused his net worth with self-worth? What is the difference between the two?
2. Do you think Joseph's brothers felt forgotten and inferior because of the way Jacob treated Joseph? Explain.

Read verses 12-36:

These verses tell the story of how Joseph's brothers sold him to Midianite merchants, who took him to Egypt and sold him to Potiphar, one of Pharaoh's officials.

3. Do you think God forgot about Joseph?

Chapter 39: Continue to read Joseph's story about his time spent in Potiphar's house.

Read verses 20-23:
These verses discuss the time Joseph was thrown into prison because of an incident with Potiphar's wife.

4.   How did God care for Joseph while he was in prison?

Chapter 45: Family Reunion

Read 45:5: God cares about your family.

5.   Do you understand why Joseph had to go through a difficult season for the benefit of his family? Explain.

REFLECT ON IT

Daily Verses

Day 1

Scripture: Hebrews 13:5-6
"...'I will never fail you. I will never abandon you.' So we can say with confidence, 'the Lord is my helper, so I will have no fear. What can mere people do to me?'" (NLT)

Observation
God has promised you that He will never fail or abandon you.

Application

How does knowing that God is your helper, ever present and vigilant, affect your outlook on the future? Your family's future?

Day 2

Scripture: 2 Timothy 1:7

"For God has not given us a spirit of fear and timidity, but of power, love, and self-discipline." (NLT)

Observation

God has given us a spirit of power, love, and self-discipline.

Application

During the times of fear and doubt in life, how has God's spirit brought your family through?

Day 3

Scripture: Matthew 6:33

"Seek the Kingdom of God above all else, and live righteously, and he will give you everything you need." (NLT)

Observation

God wants to have a relationship with each of us. He wants each person to seek Him.

Application
How do you seek God? How can your family seek God?

Day 4

Scripture: Jeremiah 29:10-13
"This is what the Lord says, 'You will be in Babylon for seventy years. But then I will come and do for you all the good things I have promised, and I will bring you home again. For I know the plans I have for you,' says the Lord. 'They are plans for good and not disaster, to give you a future and a hope. In those days when you pray, I will listen. If you look for me wholeheartedly, you will find me.'" (NLT)

Observation
God has always made Himself reachable. In today's Scripture, God explains that there will be strife, but once that time is over all things promised will be. God keeps His promises.

Application
Reflect on a time when God brought your family through strife. During that time, did you all search for God? How did that look?

Day 5

Scripture: Jeremiah 1:5
"'I knew you before I formed you in your mother's womb. Before you were born I set you apart and appointed you as my prophet to the nations.'" (NLT)

Observation
There is nothing that God does not know about each and every one of us.

Application
How does knowing that God knows everything about you affect your relationship with Him? How does that relationship affect your family?

Day 6

Summary
Use this space to write any thoughts God has put in your heart and mind about hope for your home.

BLACK FAMILIES MATTER
HOPE FOR YOUR HOME

SESSION 3

"Locating Hope for Your Home"

SUMMARY

We've all probably seen a cartoon or movie in which the characters were looking for treasure and had to dig deep in the sand or dirt to retrieve it. They're hot, sweaty, dirty, and tired, but they refused to quit until they found the treasure. Why is that? Because the treasure was valuable to them.

In today's lesson, Pastors Don and Mona talk about two key premises connected to finding hope for your home:

1. In order to find your treasure in your life, you are going to have to dig in some dirt.

2. Hope is a priceless treasure for your home, but it will get misplaced if all you see is the dirt in your home (marriage, children, etc.).

INTRODUCTION

Have you ever lost something valuable in your home? Your favorite or most expensive piece of jewelry, a picture, or keepsake that carries special meaning? You wracked your brain, trying to recall the last place you saw it, retracing your steps, asking everyone if they have seen it—all to no avail? How did you feel when you had done everything you could think to do and yet you still did not locate your treasure?

Maybe you felt frustrated. Maybe you were overcome with anger...with yourself for not taking better care of such a valuable item. But once you were resigned to the fact that you would never see this treasure again, it was difficult to regain the belief that you would ever find it.

Maybe it wasn't something tangible that you lost. We've all experienced a time when life has become overwhelming—when the stress, sadness, pain, anger, or loneliness fills every space in our lives and we lose something that is extremely valuable: HOPE.

Now, what if when you least expect it, you find your missing treasure but it is in the dirtiest, yuckiest crevice in your home? Dust, cobwebs, dead bugs, live spiders??? Is that treasure worth digging through the grime to get to it? On that same note, is it worth digging in the dirt of your life if buried within it is a treasure called HOPE?

OPEN UP

Heavenly Father, thank you for another opportunity for us to come together. We stand in agreement that we all will hear from You and learn more about how to locate hope in our homes. Help us to recognize how what we focus on in our homes determines whether or not we hold on to our hope. We want to hold on to our hope because when we do so, we are holding on to You. In Jesus's name, Amen.

1. Whether thrift shopping, mining precious gems, or digging deep into the earth to uncover a treasure chest, finding something of value usually takes a significant amount of focus, determination, and effort. Do you think people are more or less likely to apply a similar amount of energy toward unearthing the treasure in their family? What about you?
2. In the beginning of his message, Pastor Don said, "Sometimes treasure is found in the most unlikely places." Have you ever found a "treasure" when you least expected it or in a place you never thought it could be found?
3. If something can be considered valuable to a person at one point but later deemed worthless by that same person and thrown away or exchanged, what makes something valuable a treasure? Is it the same answer for people and relationships?

TAKE IT IN: DVD SESSION

Watch the DVD for this session now. We have provided a space for Notes. There you can record any key thoughts, questions, and things you want to remember or follow up on. After watching the video, have someone read the discussion questions in the "Talk It Over" section and direct the discussion among the group. As you go through each of the subsequent sections, ask someone else to read the questions and direct the discussion.

TALK IT OVER

Pastor Don has shared a lot of information around losing and locating hope in our homes. Whether we found treasure in an unlikely place, or we found it only after quite a bit of digging, hopefully we all realize that no matter our situation, there is something of value in

43

NOTES

NOTES

our lives as well. God never leaves us hopeless! Now is a great time to talk about what we have heard and share our thoughts about it. So, let's talk it over...

1. What might you find if you went on a relational treasure hunt in your home?
2. Referencing Matthew 13:44, Pastor Don talked about a man who finds treasure hidden in a field. In the Message Bible this Scripture reads, "God's kingdom is like a treasure hidden in a field for years and then accidentally found by a trespasser. The finder is ecstatic – what a find! – and proceeds to sell everything he owns to raise money and buy that field." This Scripture seems to suggest that intentionally looking for something or owning it is not as important as recognizing its value once it is discovered. What would you say was the biggest difference between the owner of the field and the trespasser who actually discovered the treasure?
3. In Matthew 13:44, the owner of the field had years, not to find the treasure but to realize its value. For all we know, the field's owner saw that same treasure but never thought that it was valuable because he couldn't see past the dirt it was surrounded by. What are some of the reasons we miss out on recognizing the valuable people in our lives? In other words, what are some of the dirt in our lives that we allow to hide our treasures?
4. What lessons can we take from this Scripture to apply to our own lives?

WALK IT OUT

Finding hope in our homes is always a choice; sometimes we make the right decision, but sometimes we cannot see anything other than dirt. When we listened to God and saw our family or circumstance with spiritual eyes, we have a story to share with others about how

LOCATING HOPE IN YOUR HOME

Read 1 Samuel 16

Samuel arrived at the house of Jesse. Jesse presents seven of his sons. Samuel sees that they are all amazing men, physically fit, well educated in Jewish law, dedicated to God, but not good enough.

1. What message did Samuel receive from God in verse 7?

Samuel asked Jesse to get his son David, who was out tending the sheep. As soon as Samuel saw David, Jesse knew that David was the one. Despite the fact that David was not physically impressive, he had what it took to be the strong leader Israel needed.

2. Who in your family might you be overlooking because of his or her physical appearance or behavior? Why?

David was thought to be 12-16 years old when he was anointed. He did not become king over Israel until he was 30 years old, and he ruled over Israel for 40 years.

YOU DON'T GET THE TREASURE WITHOUT THE DIRT

Read 1 Samuel 13:14; Acts 13:22

God considered David a man after His own heart. This does not mean that he did not sin (have dirt in his life); it means he knew how to repent.

49

332333333

33333

33333333

Read 2 Samuel 11-22: David's Downfall

These verses tell about David's adulterous affair with Bathsheba, perhaps the dirtiest sin of all; however, out of the dirt came the greatest treasure all – Jesus in the flesh (Matthew 1:1).

3. Look around you; there may be treasure in your spouse, your kids, your community, and your church, but you are not seeing it because of the dirt.

REFLECT ON IT

Daily Verses

Day 1

Scripture: Matthew 13:44
"God's kingdom is like a treasure hidden in a field for a year and then accidentally found by a trespasser. The finder is ecstatic – what a find! – and proceeds to sell everything he owns to raise money and buy that field." (MSG)

Observation
Recognizing the value of something or somebody is not a natural ability. The owner of the field doesn't recognize the treasure; it is the trespasser who sees it and buys the field in order to get the treasure.

Application
What is Jesus telling us about realizing the value of God's kingdom? How does this apply to the "dirt" in your own life?

50

Day 2

Scripture: 2 Corinthians 4:7
"But we have this treasure in earthen vessels, that the excellency of the power may be of God, and not of us." (KJV)

Observation
This Scripture teaches us that within our unsubstantial bodies of clay resides a great, precious treasure from God.

Application
If God can place such a valuable prize within us, what does that say about there being treasures in our spouses, children, and other family members?

Day 3

Scripture: Romans 8:24-25
"We were given this hope when we were saved. (If we already have something, we don't need to hope for it. But if we look forward to something we don't have yet, we must wait patiently and confidently.) (NLT)

Observation
This Scripture teaches that hope is always connected to wanting something that we don't yet have. It also shows that patiently and confidently waiting is a part of the process of getting what you are hoping for.

51

Application
Where are you in recognizing that how you wait is a significant part of the hoping process?

Day 4

Scripture: Hebrews 6:11
"Our great desire is that you will keep on loving others as long as life lasts, in order to make certain that what you hope for will come true." (NLT)

Observation
There is a connection between loving others and having the thing you are hoping for come to pass. This type of love is God-like love—enduring and long-lasting.

Application
As you meditate on this Scripture, think about how critical maintaining Godly love for your family is to bringing hope back to your home or keeping it there.

Day 5

Scripture: Deuteronomy 7:6
"For you are a holy people, who belong to the Lord your God. Of all the people on Earth, the Lord your God has chosen you to be His own special treasure." (NLT)

Observation
God chose the people of Israel to be His special people. He did this knowing all of their flaws; He did this despite their dirt.

Application

What can we take from this truth and how can we apply it to our own lives?

Day 6

Summary

Use this space to write any thoughts God has put in your heart and mind about hope for your home.

BLACK FAMILIES MATTER
HOPE FOR YOUR FAMILY

SESSION 4

"Holding on to Hope"

SUMMARY

Sometimes the calendar can make us feel like we should be further along than we actually are in our lives. Every "big" birthday, those that end with a "zero," and even those smaller ones that end with a "five" get us thinking and pondering why we are not further along than we are. If we're not careful, we'll misplace our hope looking at the clock and the calendar!

At other times, troubling circumstances can persist for so long in our lives and in our families that we can lose hope. We wonder, "Why am I going through this?" or "Will this ever change?"

In today's lesson, Pastors Don and Mona talk about these "darkroom" periods and why God sometimes allows them into our lives.

INTRODUCTION

Often, when God doesn't step in immediately to change challenging circumstances in our lives, He's trying to bring about more than mere superficial "change"; He's looking to cause transformation. Transformation is defined as "extreme, radical change." God is looking to bring this type of deep, fundamental transformation into our lives. Each time this happens, the process brings us a little closer to God's ultimate intent, making us over into the image of His Son.

During these transformational seasons of our lives, we must remain patient, vigilant, and hold on to our hope in the promises of God. Psalm 23:4-5 says, "Even though I walk through the darkest valley, I will fear no evil, for you are with me; your rod and your staff, they comfort me. You prepare a table before me in the presence of my enemies. You anoint my head with oil; my cup overflows." Even when surrounded by our enemies, we can find comfort in knowing that God is protecting and preparing something great for us.

OPEN UP

Lord, thank you for all that you've done for us during every season of our lives. As we enter into today's discussion, grant each of us the courage to openly share the struggles we face in holding on to our hope during those challenging periods of our lives when you are developing us. Even though we know that this is all a part of the process of becoming who you want us to be, it still can be a trying, uncomfortable, and painful time. Please help us to lean on each other and gain strength from the knowledge that we are not alone in our struggles. In Jesus's name, Amen.

1. Share with your group about a time when you felt hopeless and you were disappointed because you thought things would

change long before they actually did. Your experience could have involved situations such as:

a. A relationship that didn't work out
b. An uncomfortable job situation
c. A wayward child

2. During your time of hopelessness, what were your thoughts about God? Did you feel He was silent? Absent? At work in the situation?
3. In hindsight, how do you think God used your time of hopelessness to develop you?

TAKE IT IN: DVD SESSION

Watch the DVD for this session now. We have provided a space for Notes. There you can record any key thoughts, questions, and things you want to remember or follow up on. After watching the video, have someone read the discussion questions in the "Talk It Over" section and direct the discussion among the group. As you go through each of the subsequent sections, ask someone else to read the questions and direct the discussion.

TALK IT OVER

Read Psalm 23:1-6 (NIV)

"The LORD is my shepherd, I lack nothing. He makes me lie down in green pastures, he leads me beside quiet waters, he refreshes my soul. He guides me along the right paths for his name's sake. Even though I walk through the darkest valley, I will fear no evil, for you

NOTES

NOTES

are with me; your rod and your staff, they comfort me. You prepare a table before me in the presence of my enemies. You anoint my head with oil; my cup overflows. Surely your goodness and love will follow me all the days of my life, and I will dwell in the house of the LORD forever."

4. Consider a time in the past when you thought you couldn't make it but you did. In hindsight, how did God use that time to develop your character?
5. In the video, the pastors share that Psalm 23 is an example of how during the "darkroom" periods of our lives we stop talking about God and start talking to God. Why do you think that so often we wait until we are under pressure before we truly start to have real, meaningful conversations with God?
6. Describe in your own words how these verses provide encouragement to hold on to your hope during trying times.
7. The pastors also note that during challenging times God is more interested in developing our character than our comfort. What are some examples of character traits that God looks to develop in us during trying times?

WALK IT OUT

Pastor Don and Pastor Mona also compare times of development in our lives to a caterpillar in the cocoon undergoing the transformation to a butterfly. When you see a butterfly, you see a transformed creature. You don't even remember the caterpillar. God wants our families to get to a place where the things that are holding us back are gone permanently so we can move into the life He has ordained for us.

8. Share with the group something from the past that God has freed your family from. This could involve:

   a. Guilt from the past
   b. Childhood scars
   c. Unhealthy relationships
   d. Expectations of failure from others

9. How has being freed from the burden(s) you discussed in Question #8 transformed your family? In what ways is your family fundamentally different than before?
10. God has the ability to take the negative in our lives and create a positive experience. Instead of waiting on God to turn the situation around, too many times we decide to take matters into our own hands and try to resolve our problems ourselves. Think of a time when instead of waiting on God you moved forward with your own solution to a family problem. What was the outcome?

11. How do you think the situation discussed in Question #9 may have turned out differently if you had instead turned it over to God?
12. While some of our transformations are in the past, God is constantly at work within our lives, refining and developing our character. Share one way in which you feel that God is at work in your family right now in a way that may ultimately lead to your next transformation?
13. Think of a person (relative, friend, co-worker) who is currently going through a darkroom experience in his or her family. What are 1-2 practical things that you can do to be a blessing and support this person?

MOVE IT FORWARD

This week, take what you learned and spend some time putting it into practice. Choose one or more of the following activities to further your spiritual growth and even connect with others in your group. Don't feel you have to complete all of these. Decide what you can commit to and go for it. Consider sharing your experiences the next time you meet with the group.

 CIRCLES OF LIFE.
Share how you have done with inviting the people on the "Circles of Life" to church or your small group. We filled these out during Session 2.

PRAY FOR EACH OTHER THIS WEEK.
You can use the Prayer and Praise Report gathered earlier in this meeting to support your group in prayer.

REFLECT ON IT.
Commit to daily connection with God. See suggestions on how to do that each day in the "Reflect On It" section.

CHANGE YOUR MIND.
Memorizing Scripture helps to redirect our minds to God's plan. Take time to give this important practice a try. Here's a passage that highlights this week's theme; choose part or all to memorize:

Galatians 6:9 (NLT)
"So let's not get tired of doing what is good. At just the right time we will reap a harvest of blessing if we don't give up."

DEEPER STUDY

DEVELOPMENT TAKES TIME

Read Genesis 37: Joseph and His Family

1. How would you describe Joseph's relationship with his brothers?
2. Describe the sibling rivalry in your family.
3. Who is the most like Joseph?

LOOKING DEEPER

4. How do you see the sovereign hand of God at work through this chapter?
5. How do you see God's hand at work in your own life?

63

LOOKING REFLECTIVELY

God "broke" Joseph by taking him out of comfortable circumstances and stretching him. God often has to "break" us before He can use us.

6. How has God broken you?
7. How has it strengthened you?
8. Are you willing to let God do whatever He needs to in your life to make you usable to Him? Explain?

Be honest with the Lord, and ask Him to make you willing, trusting His loving and sovereign hand in your life.

REFLECT ON IT

Daily Verses

Day 1

Scripture: James 1:2-4
"Consider it pure joy, my brothers and sisters, whenever you face trials of many kinds, because you know that the testing of your faith produces perseverance. Let perseverance finish its work so that you may be mature and complete, not lacking anything." (NIV)

Observation
God often uses trials in order to bring about transformation in our lives and character, with the ultimate goal for us to become more like Christ.

Application
When we are in a "darkroom" phase of our lives, we need to press into the situation and embrace the opportunity to be transformed, holding fast to the belief that God has greater things in store for us in the end.

Day 2

Scripture: Psalm 23:1-6
"The LORD is my shepherd, I lack nothing. He makes me lie down in green pastures, he leads me beside quiet waters, he refreshes my soul. He guides me along the right paths for his name's sake. Even though I walk through the darkest valley, I will fear no evil, for you are with me; your rod and your staff, they comfort me. You prepare a table before me in the presence of my enemies. You anoint my head with oil; my cup overflows. Surely your goodness and love will follow me all the days of my life, and I will dwell in the house of the LORD forever." (NIV)

Observation
Even though we know that God uses trials for our ultimate benefit, that does not make them pleasant experiences. On the contrary, oftentimes the more radical the transformation, the more painful the trial. This makes it critical that we seek an even more intimate relationship with God during these times.

Application
Pray consistently and frequently. Lean on the promises of God. Seek an open and honest dialogue through your prayers.

Day 3

Scripture: Romans 12:2
"Do not conform to the pattern of this world, but be transformed by the renewing of your mind. Then you will be able to test and approve what God's will is—his good, pleasing and perfect will." (NIV)

Observation
Transformation is a critical element of our Christian experience. While it often pursues us through trials, we should also actively seek out opportunities for transformation.

Application
Whether you are just entering into a darkroom experience, in the midst of one, or just coming out, pursue transformation in your life through prayer, reflection on God's word, and worship.

Day 4

Scripture: Acts 19:8-10
"Paul entered the synagogue and spoke boldly there for three months, arguing persuasively about the kingdom of God. But some of them became obstinate; they refused to believe and publicly maligned the Way. So Paul left them. He took the disciples with him and had discussions daily in the lecture hall of Tyrannus. This went on for two years, so that all the Jews and Greeks who lived in the province of Asia heard the word of the Lord." (NIV)

Observation
As Christians, sometimes we will face trials because of our belief.

Application
We must not let trials and opposition discourage us from sharing our faith and living lives that witness to others.

Day 5

Scripture: 2 Corinthians 12:8-10
"Three times I pleaded with the Lord to take it away from me. But he said to me, 'My grace is sufficient for you, for my power is made perfect in weakness.' Therefore I will boast all the more gladly about my weaknesses, so that Christ's power may rest on me. That is why, for Christ's sake, I delight in weaknesses, in insults, in hardships, in persecutions, in difficulties. For when I am weak, then I am strong." (NIV)

Observation
These verses refer to the Apostle Paul's "thorn in the flesh." While the Bible does not clearly explain exactly what his thorn in the flesh was, common theories are that it may have been a physical, psychological, or spiritual aliment, or an ongoing temptation. Regardless, he did not let it prevent him from completing his mission of sharing God's Word.

Application
As we deal with darkroom experiences in our own lives, we must not let them distract us from serving others in the way that Jesus would have us to. We must stay on mission.

Day 6

Summary
Use the *following pages* to summarize any thoughts God has put in your heart and mind about the things that we have looked at during your "Reflect On It" time this week.

Day 6 (continued)

BLACK FAMILIES MATTER
HOPE FOR YOUR HOME

SESSION 5

"God Is Still on the Job"

SUMMARY

Last week you and your group talked about how we all go through dark periods in our lives in order for God to transform us into who He has called us to be. But did you know that this transformation always begins in the night, in the darkness? Genesis 1:5 says, "And God called the light Day, and the darkness He called Night. And the evening and the morning were the first day" (KJV). Note that evening came before morning in God's first day. Our days place morning before evening, but that's not God's order for the day. Why? Because God begins to work at night, never sleeping nor slumbering—He is working on our behalf always, especially in our dark seasons. Therefore, we can hold on to our hope in dark times because in God's timing, our morning is coming! "Weeping may endure for a night, but joy cometh in the morning!" (Psalm 30:5 KJV)

You can hold on to your hope because God is always at work for you and your families. He is still on the job, no matter the time of day!

INTRODUCTION

Pastors Don and Mona Brawley recount a story of when their youngest son was missing at a park near a lake and how they refused to give up searching for their son until he was found. In the news, it is not uncommon to hear reports of search and rescue missions. Oftentimes, the search parties are at it for days and even weeks to no avail. Eventually, they have to call it quits. Imagine being the one lost and feeling as if no one cares enough to find you.

There are times life may seem to beat you down to the point that you may relate to the hopelessness of being lost. At times, we wonder if we have been forgotten and left alone. We wonder if anyone cares. But God cares! He knows exactly where we are and where we have been. He will not give up on you! He will go the distance! He will bring you out! We have to remind ourselves that we are called to be prisoners of hope. God has not forgotten about you or your situation. Amid the darkness and hopelessness of the situation you face, God is still on the job. His desire is to cultivate, groom, and eventually move you from where you are to a better place.

Zechariah 9:12 reads, "Return to your stronghold, O prisoners of hope; today I declare that I will restore to you double."

OPEN UP

Lord, thank you for never leaving us or forsaking us! We are learning that in the midst of the darkest of circumstances, you are there. You are always there. We ask that you will lead our discussion and let your presence be felt throughout our time together. In Jesus's name we pray, Amen.

1. Briefly tell about a dark period you or your family went through or a time when you felt God had forgotten about you/us?

2. Looking back, share a time when you thought God had forgotten you but afterwards you realized He was there all along, working on your behalf the entire time?

TAKE IT IN: DVD SESSION

Watch the DVD for this session now. We have provided a space for Notes. There you can record any key thoughts, questions, and things you want to remember or follow up on. After watching the video, have someone read the discussion questions in the "Talk It Over" section and direct the discussion among the group. As you go through each of the subsequent sections, ask someone else to read the questions and direct the discussion.

TALK IT OUT

Much of what Pastor Mona had to say in this session revolved around God working on your behalf during the darkest times of your life. She referred to Psalm 30:5 as a basis for our hope.

Those words were most likely penned by David. They were used during Solomon's period to remind the community of Israel that personal pain and suffering will always pale in comparison to the great deliverance by our God. These words are still relevant to believers today that our God is an awesome deliverer. He will come through for you even in the darkest of situations.

3. Discuss a time when God opened or closed a door for you overnight.
4. Psalm 30:5 (KJV) reads, "Weeping may endure for a night but joy cometh in the morning." When you hear these words, what do they refer to?

NOTES

NOTES

5. What are some instances when you may have wept all night but joy came in the morning?
6. This Scripture reminds us that even in the darkest times God has not forgotten about us. How does this Scripture serve to remind you of God's faithfulness to bring you out of the dark situations in your life?
7. Pastor Mona used Matthew 14:22-27 to remind us that even in the darkest times Jesus is still in control. Why do you think Jesus told his disciples to get into the boat to cross to the other side of the lake when he knew a storm would arise?
8. What was the significance of the time that Jesus chose to come to them?
9. What were Jesus's first words to them?

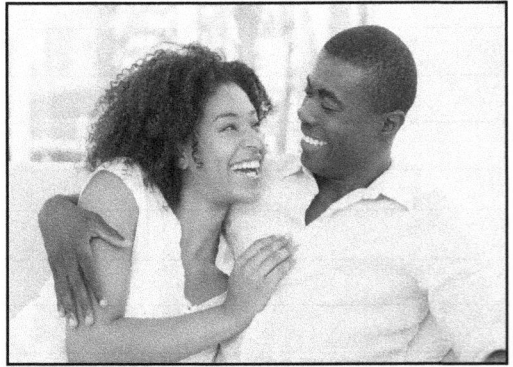

WALK IT OUT

Pastor Mona encouraged us to remember that God is always on our side and has not forgotten us. God never sleeps on the job. He is working even in the dark of night when we think our circumstances are hopeless. Zechariah 9:12 reads, "Return to your stronghold, O prisoners of hope; today I declare that I will restore to you double." This Scripture exhorts us to become prisoners of hope. As believers, our trust and hope must be in God. He is the only one that can deliver us. When we think of turning our lives from hopelessness to hopefulness we need to practice inputting hope into our seemingly hopeless situations. Our hope should be in Christ and in His power.

It is God's plan that we live productive and fulfilled lives. In an effort to not repeat some of the previous habits that have led to hopelessness we need to ponder: What did I put my hope and trust in before putting my hope in Christ? How well did that practice serve me? Leave time to reflect on these questions for a moment.

10. The Scripture in Zechariah calls us prisoners of hope. How would becoming a prisoner of hope change the way you see your family?
11. What would your life look like as a prisoner of hope in your home, on your job, in your family, from day to day?
12. What new habits will you need to put in place to build a culture of hope in your home and family?

MOVE IT FORWARD

This week, take what you learned and spend some time putting it into practice. Choose one or more of the following activities to further your spiritual growth and even connect with others in your group. Don't feel you have to complete all of these. Decide what you can commit to and go for it. Consider sharing your experiences the next time you meet with the group.

PRAY FOR EACH OTHER THIS WEEK.
You can use the Prayer and Praise Report gathered earlier in this meeting to support your group in prayer.

REFLECT ON IT.
Commit to daily connection with God. See suggestions on how to do that each day in the "Reflect On It" section.

CHANGE YOUR MIND.
Memorizing Scripture helps to redirect our minds to God's plan. Take time to give this important practice a try.

Psalm 121:4 (NASB)
"Behold, He who keeps Israel will neither slumber nor sleep."

DEEPER STUDY

GOD IS STILL ON THE JOB

Simon Peter, also known as Cephas (John 1:42), was one of the first followers of Jesus Christ. He was an outspoken and ardent disciple, one of Jesus's closest friends, an apostle, and a "pillar" of the church (Galatians 2:8). Peter was enthusiastic, strong-willed, impulsive, and, at times, brash. But for all his strengths, Peter had several failings in his life. Still, the Lord, who chose him, continued to mold him into exactly who He intended Peter to be.

Read Matthew 14:28

Peter overcomes fear. Whether stepping out of a boat onto a tossing sea or stepping across the threshold of a Gentile home for the first time, Peter found courage in following Christ. "There is no fear in love. But perfect love drives out fear..." (1 John 4:18).

1. What is your greatest fear?
2. How is God's love helping you to overcome it?

Read Matthew 26:69

Jesus forgives unfaithfulness. After he had boasted of his fidelity, Peter fervently denied the Lord three times. It seemed that Peter had burned his bridges, but Jesus lovingly rebuilt them and restored Peter to service. Peter was a former failure, but with Jesus, failure is not the end. "If we are faithless, he remains faithful, for he cannot disown himself." (2 Timothy 2:13)

78

3. Think of something you have done that caused you to think you had burned your bridges?
4. How has Jesus's love help to rebuild them?

Read John 1:42

Jesus sees us as He intends us to be. The very first time they met, Jesus called Simon "Peter." The rough and reckless fisherman was, in Jesus's eyes, a firm and faithful rock. "He who began a good work in you will carry it on to completion…" (Philippians 1:6).

5. If Jesus were to change your name, what would it be and what would it mean?

REFLECT ON IT

Daily Verses

Day 1

Scripture: Romans 5:2
"Through him we have also obtained access by faith into this grace in which we stand, and we rejoice in hope of the glory of God." (ESV)

Observation
Through Jesus Christ we have been given access to the grace of God by which we stand. We rejoice because Jesus Christ is our hope.

Application
How can your daily life reflect the knowledge that Jesus is the Hope of the Glory of God?

Day 2

Scripture: Hebrews 11:1
"Now faith is the assurance of things hoped for, the conviction of things not seen." (ESV)

Observation
You must hope in order to have faith. Faith brings assurance for the possibilities of things hoped for whether you see them or not.

Application
How can you apply faith for things hoped for in your family and daily life?

Day 3

Scripture: Romans 5:3-4
"Not only that, but we rejoice in our sufferings, knowing that suffering produces endurance, and endurance produces character, and character produces hope." (ESV)

Observation
In the midst of trying times, our trust in God produces endurance, which produces character, and that character produces hope.

Application
How do you think the relationship of suffering in your life ultimately produces hope for you and your family?

Day 4

Scripture: Hebrews 11:6
"But without faith it is impossible to please Him, for he who comes to God must believe that He is, and that He is a rewarder of those who diligently seek Him." (NKJV)

Observation
The language that moves God to act upon our behalf is faith. When we come to Him it must be with an open heart of faith believing that He is who He says He is and is more than able to accomplish what you ask Him to do in your life and family.

Application
How does faith work in relation to you obtaining God's best for your life and your family?

Day 5

Scripture: Psalm 146:5
"Happy is he who has the God of Jacob for his help, Whose hope is in the Lord his God." (NKJV)

Observation
Those who trust God for their help will be happy, not because of external circumstances but because they know God as the source of their help and hope.

Application
How does hoping in God produce happiness in your life? How will it change your family?

Day 6

Summary
Use the following space to write any thoughts God has put on your heart and mind about the things we have looked at in this session and during your "Reflect On It" time this week.

BLACK FAMILIES MATTER
HOPE FOR YOUR HOME

SESSION 6

"Lasting Hope for Your Home"

SUMMARY

Welcome to the sixth and final session of "Hope for Your Home." During the previous weeks, you and your group gained a better understanding of the meaning of hope. It is our deepest desire that each of you are now fully convinced that your family matters to God and that He is always present, giving you a reason to hope again, even after it was lost. Family is not a social institution; it was created by God to be the foundation upon which all societies are built. God wants you and your entire family to be whole—spiritually, relationally, emotionally, and financially. He also wants you and your family to be with Him for all eternity. So, open your hearts and minds to hear what it takes to have lasting hope for your home.

INTRODUCTION

Over the past several weeks, your small group has discussed the many reasons it is possible for you to have hope for your home, no matter what you may be going through. One of the most significant truths to be learned from this series is that your condition does not have to be your conclusion. 2 Corinthians 4:18 states, "So we fix our eyes not on what is seen, but on what is unseen, since what is seen is temporary, but what is unseen is eternal." In order to truly grasp the possibility of change in your circumstance, you must make sure you "fix your eyes" on God, His word, and His promises because, except for three things – faith, hope, and love—anything can change (1 Corinthians 13:13). Even the darkest of seasons and direst of circumstances will not last. Therefore, focusing on God—who is the source of our faith, hope, and love—is the one sure path to lasting hope.

OPEN UP

Lord, thank you for bringing us together for the final week of this series. We have learned so much about ourselves, your love, and how to have hope for our families. We surrender our thoughts to you and receive your wisdom and truth around maintaining hope. Fill us with your love, faith, and hope until it overflows into every area of our lives and our families. In Jesus's name we pray, Amen.

1. Does anyone have any new insights to share about how to have hope for your family?
2. Last week we talked about how God is always on the job in our lives, even in our darkest times when we cannot see evidence of it. Did this truth impact your week in any way? Share with your group.

3. Are there any hopes that have come true during this six-week series? Please share with your group.

TAKE IT IN: DVD SESSION

Watch the DVD for this session now. We have provided a space for Notes. There you can record any key thoughts, questions, and things you want to remember or follow up on. After watching the video, have someone read the discussion questions in the "Talk It Over" section and direct the discussion among the group. As you go through each of the subsequent sections, ask someone else to read the questions and direct the discussion.
NOTES

TALK IT OVER

Pastor Don shared some wonderful insights on making sure you are focused on acquiring lasting hope that will last throughout eternity. Hearing is one way we learn; discussing and sharing with each other is another. So let's talk it over and share what we gained from this session.

4. Celebrate and encourage any group member who gave his or her life to Christ. Talk about when you committed your life to Jesus and describe the sense of hope you received when you did.
5. Pastor Don said, "Your condition doesn't have to be your conclusion." Why is it important to know that your condition is not necessarily your conclusion? Why is this such an important truth to accept?
6. 1 Corinthians 13:13 reads, "And now these three remain: faith, hope and love. But the greatest of these is love." Realizing that

NOTES

NOTES

outside of faith, hope, and love, everything else changes, what have you been putting your hope in—things that will change or things eternal? Why does Pastor Don emphasize this as a key lesson?

7. Pastor Don quoted this saying, "What seems like the end of the road is only a bend in the road if you're willing to make the turn." What does this statement mean to you?

8. Consider the Eternity Rope illustration (which shows a very, very long rope where a small part of it is colored red and the rest of it is white). What do the red and white parts of the rope represent? Why is it so important to focus on the white part of the rope and not the red part?

9. The end of Psalm 30:5 reads, "...weeping may endure for a night, but joy comes in the morning." Have you been placing a period where God has placed a comma? How does seeing a comma instead of a period affect your thoughts about the seasons of weeping in your life?

WALK IT OUT

Knowledge can be simply defined as what we know while wisdom can be defined as knowing how and when to apply what we know. Moving beyond what is known and thinking deeply about how to use it in a practical way is a key step to God transforming our lives. Reflecting on moments and seasons in our lives from the perspective of this session's lessons can be truly eye-opening for us. We encourage each of you to openly share your responses to the questions in this section, with the hope that the discussion will be both enlightening and transformative.

10. Psalms 30:5 says, "...weeping may endure for the night, but joy comes in the morning." Pastor Don admonishes us not to put

a period where God has only placed a comma. Can you recall a time concerning your family when you put a period at the end of a season of weeping? What did God do to show you that He placed a comma there?

11. Charles Murray found out how much he mattered to God that night on the diving platform when he surrendered his life to the Lord. Has something ever happened to you where just how much you matter to God became real to you?

12. Charles Murray's salvation story is an amazing one. But everyone's story about the moment they surrendered all to God and accepted Jesus as their Lord and Savior is to be celebrated. Share your story about the day you gave your life to Christ and how you remember your life changing as a result of that decision.

MOVE IT FORWARD

This week, take what you learned and spend some time putting it into practice. Choose one or more of the following activities to further your spiritual growth and even connect with others in your group. Don't feel you have to complete all of these. Decide what you can commit to and go for it. Consider sharing your experiences the next time you meet with the group.

👏 PRAY FOR EACH OTHER THIS WEEK.
You can use the Prayer and Praise Report gathered earlier in this meeting to support your group in prayer.

91

REFLECT ON IT.
Commit to daily connection with God. See suggestions on how to do that each day in the "Reflect On It" section.

CHANGE YOUR MIND.
Memorizing Scripture helps to redirect our minds to God's plan. Take time to give this important practice a try.

DID YOU GIVE YOUR LIFE TO CHRIST?
We are so excited for you! Your first step is to find a Bible-based church in your area; your second step is to get baptized.

Psalm 103:17 (NIV)
"But from everlasting to everlasting the LORD's love is with those who fear him, and his righteousness with their children's children."

DEEPER STUDY

YOUR CONDITION ISN'T YOUR CONCLUSION

While the early church was growing rapidly, Saul the Pharisee was trying to destroy it. But God had other plans for Saul and dramatically turned him around to work for the kingdom of God, not against it.

Read Acts 9:1-19: Saul's Conversion

1. How would you compare your conversion to Paul's conversion?
2. How did the Lord get your attention?
3. Do you assume that some people are beyond God's reach?
4. How does this story challenge those assumptions?
5. Who is someone in your life, like Ananias, who has helped you on your journey?

6. Now that you have completed the first book in the series Black Families Matter, what is something in which your views have changed?

Political affiliation__
Public education__
How to raise kids__
The role of the church__
Who Jesus is__
Others__

REFLECT ON IT

Daily Verses

Day 1

Scripture: Psalm 30:5

"For His anger is but for a moment, His favor is for life; weeping may endure for the night, but joy comes in the morning." (NKJV)

Observation

When we believe that our condition is our conclusion, we are forgetting a key truth. Psalm 30:5 says, "...weeping may endure for a night, but joy comes in the morning." When we focus on our condition—our problems, our loss, our pain—we are misreading this Scripture. How? By putting a period where God put a comma. The most important part of this Scripture is the comma followed by the word 'but'. "..., but joy comes in the morning." That comma and the word 'but' is our promise from God that where we are now is not where or how our story will end!

Application

Reflect on this truth today; ask God to help you to truly believe that this Scripture is true for you and your family.

Day 2

Scripture: 2 Corinthians 4:18

"So we fix our eyes not on what is seen, but on what is unseen, since what is seen is temporary, but what is unseen is eternal." (NIV)

Observation
The Eternity Rope illustration (a very, very long rope where a small part of it is colored red and the rest of it is white) represents the little part that is spent living on earth and the long part representing our eternal life. Too many of us only focus on the red part of our rope, consumed by our needs and desires for money, jobs, houses, cars, travel, fame—the here and now, or what is "seen." Instead, our time and energy should be spent determining where we will spend the white part of the rope—or eternity, what is "unseen."

Application
As you meditate on this Scripture, ask yourself, "What have I been fixing my eyes on?"

Day 3

Scripture: 1 Corinthians 13:13
"And now these three remain: faith, hope and love. But the greatest of these is love." (NIV)

Observation
We recognize God as the source of faith and love; therefore, it is easy to imagine them as lasting throughout eternity. However, we may not as easily envision hope as something that will never change or go away.

Application
As you read and think about this Scripture, think about the significance of hope being included in this trio of everlasting precepts. Ask God how to demonstrate eternal hope for your family.

Day 4

Scripture: Romans 5:3-4
"Not only so, but we also glory in our sufferings, because we know that suffering produces perseverance; perseverance, character; character, hope." (NIV)

Observation
We often imagine being hopeful as a happy, joyful state; yet this Scripture clearly shows that hope is the result of going through a process that begins with suffering.

Application
Pray that God helps you embrace the struggle that precedes the emergence of hope for your family.

Day 5

Scripture: Romans 5:5
"And hope does not put us to shame, because God's love has been poured out into our hearts through the Holy Spirit, who has been given to us." (NIV)

Observation
This Scripture follows the one you read on Day 4. We can see how it might be possible to feel shame about being hopeful after experiencing suffering; indeed the world would expect us to live in shame over what we have experienced. However, the pouring of God's love into our hearts prevents us from feeling shame for going through this process.

Application
Pray and ask God how to use the love He has poured into your heart to diminish any shame you may be carrying as result of choices and actions you have made concerning your family.

Day 6

Scripture: Psalm 71:14
"As for me, I will always have hope; I will praise you more and more." (NIV)

Summary
Use the following space to summarize any thoughts God has put in your heart and mind about the things that we have looked at during your "Reflect On It" time this week.

CITATIONS

[1]U.S. Census Bureau, Current Population Survey, March and Annual Social and Economic Supplements, 2015 and earlier.

[2]Ricketts, E. The Origin of Black Female-Headed Families. Focus; vol 12 no 1. Institute for Research on Poverty, University of Wisconsin. 1989

[3]Martin JA, Hamilton BE, Osterman MJK, Curtin SC, Mathews TJ. Births: Final Data for 2013. National vital statistics reports; vol 64 no 1. Hyattsville, MD: National Center for Health Statistics. 2015.

[4]Carson, E.A. (2015). Prisoners in 2014. Washington, D.C.: Bureau of Justice Statistics.

[5]U.S. Department of Commerce, Census Bureau, American Community Survey (ACS), 2013. *See Digest of Education Statistics, 2014, table 102.60.*

98

WERE YOU BLESSED THROUGH
"HOPE FOR YOUR HOME"?
WE'D LOVE TO HEAR YOUR STORY.
EMAIL US AT
CANAANLANDCHURCHINTERNATIONAL@GMAIL.COM
OR POST ON OUR FACEBOOK PAGE
(CANAAN LAND CHURCH INT)

APPENDICES
RESOURCES TO MAKE YOUR SMALL GROUP EXPERIENCE EVEN BETTER!

FREQUENTLY ASKED QUESTIONS

What do we do on the first night of our group?

Like all fun things in life—have a party! A "get to know you" coffee, dinner, or dessert is a great way to launch a new study. You may want to review the Group Agreement (page 104) and share the names of a few friends you can invite to join you. But most importantly, have fun before your study time begins.

Where do we find new members for our group?

This can be tricky, especially for new groups that have only a few people or for existing groups that lose a few people along the way. We encourage you to pray with your group and then brainstorm a list of people from work, church, your neighborhood, your children's school, family, the gym, and so forth. Then have each group member invite several of the people on his or her list. Another good strategy is to ask church leaders to make an announcement or allow a bulletin insert.

No matter how you find members, it's vital that you stay on the lookout for new people to join your group. All groups tend to go through healthy attrition—the result of moves, releasing new leaders, ministry opportunities, and so forth—and if the group gets too small, it could be at risk of shutting down. If you and your group stay open, you'll be amazed at the people God sends your way. The next person just might become a friend for life. You never know!

How long will this group meet?

Most groups meet weekly for at least their first six weeks, but every other week can work as well. We strongly recommend that the group meet for the first six months on a weekly basis if at all possible. This allows for continuity, and if people miss a meeting they aren't gone for a whole month.

At the end of this study, each group member may decide if he

101

or she wants to continue on for another study. Some groups launch relationships for years to come, and others are stepping-stones into another group experience. Either way, enjoy the journey.

Can we do this study on our own?

Absolutely! This may sound crazy, but one of the best ways to do this study is not with a full house but with a few friends. You may choose to gather with another couple who would enjoy some relational time (perhaps going to the movies or having a quiet dinner) and then walking through this study. Jesus will be with you even if there are only two of you (Matthew 18:20).

What if this group is not working for us?

You're not alone! This could be the result of a personality conflict, life stage differences, geographical distance, different levels of spiritual maturity, or any number of things. Relax. Pray for God's direction, and at the end of this six-week study, decide whether to continue with this group or find another. You don't typically buy the first car you look at or marry the first person you date, and the same goes with a group. However, don't bail out before the six weeks are up—God might have something to teach you. Also, don't run from conflict or prejudge people before you have given them a chance. God is still working in your life, too!

Who is the leader?

Most groups have an official leader. But ideally, the group will mature and members will rotate the leadership of meetings. We have discovered that healthy groups rotate hosts/leaders and homes on a regular basis. This model ensures that all members grow, give their unique contribution, and develop their gifts. This study guide and the Holy Spirit can keep things on track even when you rotate leaders. Christ has promised to be in your midst as you gather. Ultimately, God is your leader each step of the way.

How do we handle the childcare needs in our group?

Very carefully. Seriously, this can be a sensitive issue. We suggest that you empower the group to openly brainstorm solutions. You may try one option that works for a while and then adjust over time. Our favorite approach is for adults to meet in the living room or dining room and to share the cost of a babysitter (or two) who can watch the kids in a different part of the house. This way, parents don't have to be away from their children all evening when their children are too young to be left at home. A second option is to use one home for the kids and a second home (close by or a phone call away) for the adults. A third idea is to rotate the responsibility of providing a lesson or care for the children either in the same home or in another home nearby. This can be an incredible blessing for kids. Finally, the most common solution is to decide that you need to have a night to invest in your spiritual lives individually or as a couple and to make your own arrangements for childcare. No matter what decision the group makes, the best approach is to dialogue openly about both the problem and the solution.

SMALL GROUP AGREEMENT

OUR PURPOSE

To provide a predictable environment where participants experience authentic community and spiritual growth.

OUR VALUES

Group Attendance
: To give priority to the group meeting. We will call or e-mail if we will be late or absent. (Completing the Group Calendar on page 105 will minimize this issue.)

Safe Environment
: To help create a safe place where people can be heard and feel loved. (Please, no quick answers, snap judgments, or simple fixes.)

Respect Differences
: To be gentle and gracious to people with different spiritual maturity, personal opinions, temperaments, or "imperfections" in fellow group members. We are all works in progress.

Confidentiality
: To keep anything that is shared strictly confidential and within the group, and to avoid sharing improper information about those outside the group.

Encouragement for Growth
: To be not just takers but givers of life. We want to spiritually multiply our lives by serving others with our God-given gifts.

Shared Ownership
: To remember that every member is a minister and to ensure that each attendee will share a small team role or responsibility over time.

Rotating Hosts/ Leaders and Homes
: To encourage different people to host the group in their homes and to rotate the responsibility of facilitating each meeting. (See the Group Calendar on page 105.)

OUR EXPECTATIONS

- Refreshments/mealtimes _____
- Childcare _____
- When we will meet (day of week) _____
- Where we will meet (place) _____
- We will begin at (time) _____ and end at _____
- We will do our best to have some or all of us attend a worship service together. Our primary worship service time will be _____
- Date of this agreement _____
- Date we will review this agreement again _____
- Who (other than the leader) will review this agreement at the end of this study _____

SMALL GROUP CALENDAR

Planning and scheduling can help ensure the greatest participation at every meeting. At the end of each meeting, review this calendar. Be sure to include a regular rotation of host homes and leaders, and don't forget birthdays, socials, church events, holidays, and mission/ministry projects.

Date	Lesson	Host Home	Dessert/Meal	Leader
Monday, October 5	1	John and Tracy's	Joshua	Sarah

SPIRITUAL PARTNERS' CHECK-IN

Briefly check in each week and write down your personal plans and progress targets for the next week (or even for the next few weeks). This could be done before or after the meeting, on the phone, through an e-mail message, or even in person from time to time.

My Name:

Spiritual Partner's Name:

WEEK	OUR PLANS	OUR PROGRESS
WEEK 1		
WEEK 2		
WEEK 3		
WEEK 4		
WEEK 5		
WEEK 6		

S.O.A.P. Bible Study Method

Scripture

Take a verse or passage, pray over it, and then read through slowly. Read through it several times. Allow God to speak to you. When reading a large passage, God will direct your attention to a certain verse or section. Write these down in your workbook or journal and focus your study there.

Observation

What is God saying in this Scripture? To search out the meaning of a verse or passage is like detective work. Is there a declaration of truth, a promise? Is there a command or exhortation? Is there a warning? Record your observations. Paraphrase and write this Scripture down in your own words in your journal. Ask, "How would I explain the Scripture if I were teaching it to someone else?"

Application

After you have done your observations and made your findings as to what the verse(s) is/are saying, you move on to application. You ask the next question, "What does this (your observations) mean for me? How does this affect my life? Does God have instructions for me today? Encouragement? Correction? Write down in your WORKBOOK God's personal message to you. "What's the ONE THING You want me to apply here God?" or "What's one thing I learned about who God is?"

Prayer

Ask for His help in accepting and applying what has been revealed. That is the kind of question that God guarantees He will answer. "Now this is the confidence we have in Him, that if we ask anything according to His will, He hears us. And if we know that He hears us, whatever we ask, we know that we have the petitions that we have asked of Him." 1 John 5: 14-15 (NIV).

PRAYER AND PRAISE REPORT

WEEK	PRAYER	PRAISE REPORT
WEEK 1		
WEEK 2		
WEEK 3		
WEEK 4		
WEEK 5		
WEEK 6		

SMALL GROUP ROSTER

NAME	PHONE NUMBER	E-MAIL

SMALL GROUP
LEADERS
RESOURCES

HOSTING AN OPEN HOUSE

If you're starting a new group, try planning an "open house" before your first formal group meeting. Even if you have only two to four core members, it's a great way to break the ice and to consider prayerfully who else might be open to joining you over the next few weeks. You can also use this kick-off meeting to hand out study guides, spend some time getting to know each other, discuss each person's expectations for the group, and briefly pray for each other.

A simple meal or good desserts always make a kick-off meeting more fun.

After people introduce themselves and share how they ended up being at the meeting (you can play a game to see who has the wildest story!), have everyone respond to a few icebreaker questions:

- What is your favorite family vacation?
- What is one thing you love about your church/our community?
- What are three things about your life growing up that most people here don't know?

Next, ask everyone to tell what he or she hopes to get out of the study. You might want to review the Small Group Agreement and talk about each person's expectations and priorities.

Finally, set an open chair (maybe two) in the center of your group and explain that it represents someone who would enjoy or benefit from this group but who isn't here yet. Ask people to pray about inviting someone to join the group over the next few weeks. Hand out postcards and have everyone write an invitation or two. Don't worry about ending up with too many people; you can always have one discussion circle in the living room and another in the dining room after you watch the lesson. Each group could then report prayer requests and progress at the end of the session.

You can skip this kick-off meeting if your time is limited, but you'll experience a huge benefit if you take the time to connect with each other in this way.

111

LEADING FOR THE FIRST TIME

Sweaty palms are a healthy sign. The Bible says God is gracious to the humble. Remember who is in control; the time to worry is when you're not worried. Those who are soft in heart (and sweaty palmed) are those whom God is sure to speak through.

Seek support. Ask your leader, co-leader, or close friend to pray for you and prepare with you before the session. Walking through the study will help you anticipate potentially difficult questions and discussion topics.

Bring your uniqueness to the study. Lean into who you are and how God wants you to uniquely lead the study.

Prepare. Prepare. Prepare. Go through the session several times. If you are using the DVD, listen to the teaching segment and Leadership Lifter. Go to www.lifetogether.com and download pertinent files. Consider writing in a journal or fasting for a day to prepare yourself for what God wants to do. Don't wait until the last minute to prepare.

Ask for feedback so you can grow. Perhaps in an e-mail or on cards handed out at the study, have everyone write down three things you did well and one thing you could improve on. Don't get defensive. Instead, show an openness to learn and grow.

Use online resources. Go to www.lifetogether.com and listen to Brett Eastman share the weekly Leadership Lifter and download any additional notes or ideas for your session. You may also want to subscribe to the Doing Life Together newsletter and LLT Newsletter. Both can be obtained for free by signing up at www.lifetogether.com/subscribe.

Prayerfully consider launching a new group. This doesn't need to happen overnight, but God's heart is for this to take place over time. Not all Christians are called to be leaders or teachers, but we are all called to be "shepherds" of a few someday.

Share with your group what God is doing in your heart. God is searching for those whose hearts are fully His. Share your trials and victories. We promise that people will relate.

Prayerfully consider whom you would like to pass the baton to next week. It's only fair. God is ready for the next member of your group to go on the faith journey you just traveled. Make it fun, and expect God to do the rest.

LEADERSHIP TRAINING 101

Congratulations! You have responded to the call to help shepherd Jesus's flock. There are few other tasks in the family of God that surpass the contribution you will be making. As you prepare to lead, whether it is one session or the entire series, here are a few thoughts to keep in mind. We encourage you to read these and review them with each new discussion leader before he or she leads.

1. **Remember that you are not alone**. God knows everything about you, and He knew that you would be asked to lead your group. Remember that it is common for all good leaders to feel that they are not ready to lead. Moses, Solomon, Jeremiah, and Timothy were all reluctant to lead. God promises, "Never will I leave you; never will I forsake you" (Hebrews 13:5). Whether you are leading for one evening, for several weeks, or for a lifetime, you will be blessed as you serve.

2. **Don't try to do it alone**. Pray right now for God to help you build a healthy leadership team. If you can enlist a co-leader to help you lead the group, you will find your experience to be much richer. This is your chance to involve as many people as you can in building a healthy group. All you have to do is call and ask people to help. You'll probably be surprised at the response.

3. **Just be yourself**. If you won't be you, who will? God wants you to use your unique gifts and temperament. Don't try to do things

exactly like another leader; do them in a way that fits you! Just admit it when you don't have an answer, and apologize when you make a mistake. Your group will love you for it, and you'll sleep better at night!

4. **Prepare for your meeting ahead of time**. Review the session and the leader's notes, and write down your responses to each question. Pay special attention to exercises that ask group members to do something other than engage in discussion. These exercises will help your group live what the Bible teaches, not just talk about it. Be sure you understand how an exercise works, and bring any necessary supplies (such as paper and pens) to your meeting. If the exercise employs one of the items in the appendix, be sure to look over that item so you'll know how it works. Finally, review "Outline for Each Session" so you'll remember the purpose of each section in the study.

5. **Pray for your group members by name**. Before you begin your session, go around the room in your mind and pray for each member by name. You may want to review the prayer list at least once a week. Ask God to use your time together to touch the heart of every person uniquely. Expect God to lead you to whomever He wants you to encourage or challenge in a special way. If you listen, God will surely lead!

6. **When you ask a question, be patient.** Someone will eventually respond. Sometimes people need a moment or two of silence to think about the question. Keep in mind, if silence doesn't bother you, it won't bother anyone else. After someone responds, affirm the response with a simple "thanks" or "good job." Then ask, "How about somebody else?" or "Would someone who hasn't shared like to add anything?" Be sensitive to new people or reluctant members who aren't ready to say, pray, or do anything. If you give them a safe setting, they will blossom over time.

7. **Provide transitions between questions.** When guiding the discussion, always read aloud the transitional paragraphs and the questions. Ask the group if anyone would like to read the paragraph or Bible passage. Don't call on anyone, but ask for a volunteer, and then be patient until someone begins. Be sure to thank the person who reads aloud.

8. **Break up into small groups each week or they won't stay.** If your group has more than seven people, we strongly encourage you to have the group gather sometimes in discussion circles of three or four people during the "Talk it Over" and "Walk it Out" sections of the study. With a greater opportunity to talk in a small circle, people will connect more with the study, apply more quickly what they're learning, and ultimately get more out of it. A small circle also encourages a quiet person to participate and tends to minimize the effects of a more vocal or dominant member. It can also help people feel more loved in your group. When you gather again at the end of the section, you can have one person summarize the highlights from each circle. Small circles are also helpful during prayer time. People who are unaccustomed to praying aloud will feel more comfortable trying it with just two or three others. Also, prayer requests won't take as much time, so circles will have more time to actually pray. When you gather back with the whole group, you can have one person from each circle briefly update everyone on the prayer requests. People are more willing to pray in small circles if they know that the whole group will hear all the prayer requests.

9. **Rotate facilitators weekly.** At the end of each meeting, ask the group who should lead the following week. Let the group help select your weekly facilitator. You may be perfectly capable of leading each time, but you will help others grow in their faith and gifts if you give them opportunities to lead. You can use the Small Group Calendar to fill in the names of all meeting leaders at once if you prefer.

116

10. **One final challenge (for new or first-time leaders): Before your first opportunity to lead, look up each of the five passages listed below**. Read each one as a devotional exercise to help you develop a shepherd's heart. Trust us on this one. If you do this, you will be more than ready for your first meeting.

Matthew 9:36
1 Peter 5:2-4
Psalm 23
Ezekiel 34:11-16
1 Thessalonians 2:7-8, 11-12

ABOUT DR. DON BRAWLEY III

Dr. Don Brawley III is a Leadership Strategist who helps influencers reach their dreams faster. He is the founder and CEO of Influencers Global, a company committed to helping leaders increase their influence, income, and impact for God's Kingdom. He along with his wife Mona are the founding pastors of Canaan Land Church International, a thriving ministry in suburban Atlanta, Georgia.

Dr. Brawley earned his Master's of Organizational Leadership (2004) and Doctorate in Strategic Leadership, with a coaching emphasis (2008), from Regent University's School of Global Leadership and Entrepreneurship.

Dr. Brawley travels nationally and abroad consulting and coaching pastors, marketplace and non-profit leaders, facilitating leadership roundtables, and delivering motivational, practical and inspiring messages. He's a highly sought-after consultant, coach, and conference speaker. He's trained leaders for Fortune 500 companies such as UPS and educational institutions such as The University of Phoenix.

Additionally, Dr. Brawley has published several works. He co-authored, Weathering the Storm: Leading in Uncertain Times with Dr. Samuel R. Chand. The book has become a favorite on four continents and has recently been translated to Portuguese.

In March 2015, he was honored, with a resolution, by the Georgia House of Representatives for his leadership accomplishments. Later in 2015, Dr. Brawley made history when he held the first ever global online conference in the Kingdom spanning 6 days across 3 continents.

Dr. Brawley has been married to his high school sweetheart Mona for over 27 years. Together they are the proud parents of three children: Brandon (Kristie), Chantelle, and Aaron.

For more information concerning Dr. Don Brawley, you may visit www.canaanlandchurch.org | www.influencersglobal.com |

Influencers Publishing, LLC is a print and digital publishing company that "nurtures the author within the influencer." Influencers Publishing is comprised of a diverse team possessing over 60 years of writing, editing, publishing, graphic design, and project management experience. The company was established by Dr. Don Brawley III and is located in Atlanta, Georgia.

𝒾NFLUENCERS 📖 PUBLISHING
www.influencerspublishing.com

119